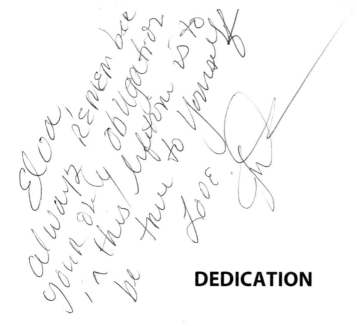

DEDICATION

To the many survivors who endured, escaped, and have not forgotten what it was like behind the sacred walls of the Roloff Fundamentalist Reform homes in Texas from 1976 thru 1983 that were meant to "teach the way of the Lord and cast out the demons of sin from within". May our stories be heard and may we always continue to fight for change. I am sharing their words, their experiences, as unique and individual as they are to each of them.

CONTENTS

INTRODUCTION

You hear about abuse in third world countries, communist camps, and reform like prisons for out of control teens and adults in need of regulation and control, but you don't often hear about it in your own communities, neighborhoods and states, but it exists. What am I referring to? Group homes, religious institutions, Bible-based boarding schools, whatever you want to name them, it all boils down to prison camps that use the Fundamentalist Baptist belief in harsh discipline, conformity, and ultimate submission of will to fulfill a purpose.

What is their purpose? To use brainwashing tactics and abusive conduct to force conformity and a belief that without total submission to the will of "God" as the leaders of their organization feel is appropriate, is met.

This comes with a price, not only emotionally but financially. Thousands of supporters of the "mission to reform" donate millions a year to these organizations, even politicians, have contributed or turned a blind eye to what is going on in America.

Parents all over the country seek to find methods to control their wayward youth and are coerced into sending them to these facilities in hopes to make them good Christians and dedicated to God and not fall prey to sin. The majority of the survivors I have interviewed and spoken to had committed no major criminal offense, if anything illegal at all, but merely done what a typical teenager does as part of growing up and making choices. The majority of misgivings could have been remedied by grounding, love and basic discipline. We all make choices in life that may or may not lead to needing some outside assistance in guiding us from being "out of control", but to force a child to be deprived of their basic human rights, be beaten into submission, brainwashed into believing there is only one means to prevent an inevitable existence in a burning hell, and even in some instances have their very innocence stolen from them by forcible rape and sexual abuse is unacceptable.

In this book you will find stories of survivors, in their own words, and unedited. They are all survivors of the Roloff Ministries Homes, centered around the Peoples Baptist Church, Corpus Christi, Texas in the 1970's and 80's. Thanks to the Constitution of the United States and the laws protecting Journalists and the identities of their sources, I am only sharing their stories by first name. Many of the survivors still live in fear of the money and powerful political affiliations associated with the many homes. One day we hope that fear will subside, but as long as money and politics go hand in hand, a child's rights to protection under the law will never mean as much as Separation of Church and State laws being abused, and used as a means to allow this to continue. Many of these organizations demand loyalty to any politician that will turn a blind eye to what goes on *"Behind Sacred Walls"*.

Peoples Baptist Church

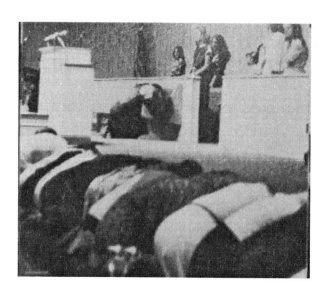

Hundreds weekly flocked to bow down on the altar in repentance for fear of damnation to hell.

To this day, I wonder if Lester Roloff knew exactly what went on behind the walls of the homes he founded. Then reality sets in and I am reminded, all the secrets, we were forced to keep in the Fundamentalist home I was raised in, and the reform homes, whose doors I entered over the years... They knew, they didn't care, it was money in the name of their God.

How could they not?

The Homes were Listed as:

- Anchor Home for Boys ages 9-17
- Lighthouse Home for Men
- Rebekah Home for Girls ages 9-17
- Jubilee Home for Women
- City of Refuge home for Older men
- Peaceful Valley Home for Retirees

I am sure it is hard to fathom why some grown adults would commit themselves to these facilities as a means of rehabilitation, but some people become destitute and are coerced by churches and family to attend to seek what is "missing or wrong" in their lives. The majority have no alternatives and succumb. What I do not understand is after hearing their stories, and trying to comprehend, why as an adult were some forcibly detained against their will when they want to leave? There are also stories of adults forcibly sent there under restraint by family members. I remember what that was like after I had graduated from High School and was a legal adult by Texas law and was forcibly restrained and locked up in my third facility at Jubilee Home.

2~DAVID T - ANCHOR HOME FOR BOYS
1982

It was a hot June Friday in Midwestern Texas in 1982. School was out for the year and I was looking forward to a nice summer of fun, family vacations and swimming. Little did I know my parents had a different summer in mind.

I learned that I was going to repeat the seventh grade when the school resumed next fall and I was not looking forward to that. I was going to make the best of the summer despite the threat of punishment from my father for my actions during the academic year. I was a rebel at heart and spent more time trying to defy the rules of the "Christian" school I had to attend, and less time studying. My father was the minister of the church where the school was located, and I was often reminded that my behavior was a bad reflection on his status within the church community. I assumed that meant I would have to spend the majority of the summer working around the church or mowing lawns for parishioners as punishment. I liked mowing lawns because it got me out of the house and away from my bible thumping father and my scornful mother who reminded me all too often that I was most likely a mirror image of Satan.

That Friday evening my father sat me down and told me that we were going on vacation, and that while we were on vacation, he was going to drop me off at a boys camp where I can learn to get closer to God, and have fun spending time with boys my age riding horses and working on a farm, and lots of fishing off the Inter-coastal waterway. This sounded great, minus the "getting close to God" part, but if it meant horses and animals I was game. He said we would be leaving the following Monday and I needed to spend my weekend packing for "camp". I loved animals and had always thought being on a farm would be cool. Little did I know…. This was only a dream.

Monday arrived, and the family loaded the car. My sister who was seven was sitting in back with me and my parents up front, whispering a lot and looking at me in the rear view mirror often. It gave me a queasy feeling, I didn't understand at that moment, but I would soon learn why. Dad didn't say much as he drove down the highway, and mom looked as if she had tears in her eyes. We drove several hours and then arrived at this group of buildings, some with fences around them and one was a church. It said Peoples Baptist Church and another sign on a small shack that looked like a ticket booth at a parking garage at the entrance that read "welcome to Roloff Ministries". I think they mislabeled the sign. After spending almost a year there, I learned it should have been labeled "Welcome to the gates of Hell", because, what happened to me after my parent dumped me into the hands of that place, was surely not anything better than hell on earth.

I was ushered into a building and told I was to be taken to the boys home from there. My dad and mom went into a room with some tall gentleman and I was told to sit in a chair by the wall next to this man that smelled like he had not bathed in several weeks. I sat there for about an hour and had to use the bathroom so bad I started to squirm. The man gave me a stern look and said, "Sit still or you will get a licking". I said, "I have to pee." He said, you ask to use the restroom, and use it only when allowed, the word PEE is forbidden". Then he motioned for me to follow him and he led me to a restroom and proceeded to stand there and expected me to pee right in front of him. I protested and he said until I can be trusted, I cannot pee alone. That was one of many moments to come that would fuel anger in me so deep, that a hatred for religion and the fundamentalist movement would create in me that lasted a few decades.

I was escorted back to my chair just in time to see my mother exit to the car quickly crying and my father returning with my suitcase, hugging me and telling me' "this will be good for me and good-bye". The man he had met with earlier in the room with my mom then spoke up and said, "Hug your father and we will be taking you over to Anchor Home, and you will not see him for a year". My heart sank into my feet. My mom didn't even stay in the building to tell me good-bye, and my dad seemed as smug as he always did when he was preaching his Sunday sermons from the pulpit. "A year?" I protested, and yelled. "This was only supposed to be a summer camp". I was promptly told to hush and not talk until spoken to or asked a question. So angrily I sank back into the chair, and cried.

I was taken in a car over to Anchor Home for Boys, where I was introduced to Bro. and Mrs. Schumacher. I passed a few other boys close to my age in the hallway, dressed in trousers, white shirts and ties, and it wasn't even a Sunday. Everyone was wearing exactly the same thing, same color, and their hair was all cut exactly the same. How could they tell anyone apart, I thought to myself?

I was told a list of rules and they took my suitcase from me and told me they had to go through it to check to make sure I did not have anything bad in my things. What can I have that was bad? I was the son of a preacher, and didn't own anything really except clothes, a few comic books and a slingshot. I had never heard so many rules.... NO television, no radio, no cussing or slang words, no talking about things we did at home before we got there, no talking about girls, no singing songs except hymns about God, and the rules went on and on.... This was not a camp or a farm, this was truly a prison, and I knew I was going to hate it.

The colored shirts my mom and I packed, were not allowed, and my blue jeans were only to be worn on days we worked in fields, or fishing for food. So they gave me some trousers and white shirts. The trousers were too big and I had to safety pin them to stay up, even with a belt. The white shirts were faded and discolored, as if someone never properly washed the sweat stains out of them, and sure didn't smell as nice as the ones my mom always washed and ironed on Saturdays. I felt like an orphan every time I had to get dressed. Then wear a tie every day? A stupid tie at that! Blue with red and white stripes and a bible and the words ACE on them. It was an eyesore for anyone. I hated even looking at myself in the mirror when I would get dressed.

I spent the first few weeks with a "buddy" because all new boys had to have someone stay with them to make sure they did not run away. After my first few "lickings", that were actually beatings with a board until my butt turned red as fire, I couldn't understand why someone would want to run away for fear of being beaten to near death, or even worse, be sent to that room at the end of a hall everyone whispered about.

Seven days a week we were forced to wake up early, pray, eat crappy food, work, pray and praise this place for how it had taught us that we are all servants of God and unworthy of love he bestowed upon us. We were to praise some man "Lester Roloff", who was the lead man of God and was in charge of seeing we leave our devilish ways behind. We went to church 4 times a week at the Peoples Baptist Church and sat in a section all our own. We were supposed to always keep our eyes in front of us, and several times I was punished later for looking around. I did notice several sections that had girls in it and older boys and older ladies. I later found out that there were other homes for people who were "lost and in need of God".

I tried my best for several months to stay out of trouble. I met a friend named Craig who told me, if we play along, we can maybe go home sooner. I knew it was going to be hard to do, but I just could not take a whole year of this place. Like I said, I tried. That did not always work. It seemed like even the simplest mistakes landed me into a world of trouble, beatings, and punishments that would make a person's jaw drop in disbelief.

I was working one day in the kitchen, and had cut my hand while cutting up vegetables for some stew they were making for supper, and swore. I didn't mean to swear, it just hurt so bad and was bleeding on my already stained shirt and I knew I would be in trouble for getting it dirtier. I was really in hot water and knew it when I was drug out of the kitchen and beaten with a paddle about 25 times, and refused to cry. I held it in, I was angry because it was not like I had cut myself on purpose. Then I was forced to kneel on a 2x4 for an hour and not move. By the time I was done my knees hurt so bad I could not stand up. Two staff members came to carry me to my bunk and I was allowed to rest for a few minutes before I had to go back to work.

Fall came and went, and I attended their school, which I really would not call a school. We did work in the paper booklets called paces, and then took tests. We sat in desks with dividers and there were no teachers except the monitors who came by to make sure we were working on something. I really don't remember learning anything except "no cheating, by memorizing the answer keys when we graded our own work", "always raise your flag to leave desk" and "never talk to someone at another desk."

November came and went and December was here. We were told we would maybe get to have a present sent by our parents, who we only got to speak to on the phone one time a month for 10 minutes, and they listened to everything we said. I was hoping instead of a present that my mom would come and get me. The last phone conversation I had with my parents, my mom said she was leaving my dad and they were getting a divorce. Then the staff took the phone away from me, and told me I should pray for my mother because she was destroying the sanctity of marriage. I was informed I was no longer allowed to talk to her on the phone and was only to receive communication from my father. I was heartbroken. Even though she was married to my dad, she was always much nicer and less harsh when I would misbehave at home. I loved and missed her dearly and always thought dad forced her to let me go to this awful place.

December 15 of 1983, my Christmas wish came true. I was pulled out of the school classroom and told to go straight to the dorm and pack my belongings and talk to no one. I ran as fast as I could and threw just my underwear in a bag and went to the office. Sure enough my mom was standing there with papers in her hands and a police officer. I learned that my mom was awarded custody of me and I was going home to live with her in her new place. I was free.

My mom and I both cried all the way home. We did not talk much about the Anchor Home or what happened behind those doors, and I think it was a good thing. She kept apologizing for letting my father send me there, and it always brought tears to her eyes and I didn't want to make her feel any worse. She came and rescued me and that was enough.

Over two decades had passed and my mother's health had taken a turn for the worse, cancer had eaten away at her organs and we started spending time together talking about my childhood, my two failed marriages, and the scattered adult life I was living. My mother asked me to tell her what happened to me at Anchor Home that had changed me because she felt I was never the same after she came and got me. I didn't have the heart to tell her I was repeatedly beaten, kicked in the groin, called names, forced to do manual labor and brainwashed into thinking I was to have no thoughts of my own, but only thoughts of God. She was suffering enough with her pain and illness.

It has been a year since my mother passed, and I was going through some old items I found in her home, and I came across an old letter addressed to me, stuck in the back of her old Bible. It Read..

My Dearest David,

I cannot tell you in words how sorry I am for the abuse you endured in that home. I know you have never spoken of it, but I have heard about them homes from other people and know they were shut down for abuse. I hope one day you can find it in your heart to forgive me for letting your father send you there. I love you with all my heart and hope that one day you can find peace in your soul and reach out and find other people that experienced what you did and find some healing in your heart. One day maybe you can find peace and forgiveness for what happened. I love you.

Mom

I have mom. I have forgiven, but I have not forgotten. I have shared my story in hopes to help others realize that some of these homes meant to reform kids, do not reform them. They create robotic followers of a religion taken to extremes for profit. I do not talk to my father, and to this day am not even sure where he is since he left the Church in Texas. I do know that I have finally gotten back on track with my life and after reaching out to a survivor I found online, living in Missouri and hearing her story, I learned I am one of thousands, I am a survivor. It does get better once you start healing and talking about it and deprogram yourself. You have to realize that you're not the worthless person you feel you are just because years ago someone brainwashed you into believing you were. I still have nightmares.

Anchor Home 1982

3~LIZ-JUBILEE HOME FOR WOMEN
1983

Have you ever had an experience that was so traumatic that it seems like after it has ended, it is a recurring nightmare that haunts you almost every night when you lay your head down to rest? I do, and until I finally met another survivor, that I was able to finally come to terms with the fact, I am a victim. I did not deserve what happened to me. Let me tell you my story.

It was the fall of 1983. I had dropped out of high school and ran away from home in my senior year. I was tired of my parents' rules, church and all the restrictions placed on me. I wanted to be "free" like the other kids I went to high school with, and not looked at as a freak or outcast for not being able to participate in all the things they did. I was not allowed to go to any school dances, or hang out at the mall. In my parents' eyes, that was sinful and doing so would be allowing the devil to control my life. I was so tired of being "different" in the eyes of my peers, isolated from all the things my classmates laughed about and enjoyed. I was 18, so I decided to run away from home.

I lasted bouncing from friend to friend's homes for about 6 months, then a shelter for young adults, then living on the streets. I got a job at a gas station, and tried to find answers in what was missing in my life. I seemed to never find happiness in anything I did. There was always something missing. I kept working and searching, then one day I found what made me happy. I met a girl, she was a great person, and we had so many common interests and fell in love. Yes, a girl, I had discovered that, although I grew up being told I would burn in hell for being homosexual, I was a lesbian and I was happy. No one or any religion was going to take this new found happiness from me. We spent 2 years together, both working, content and starting a great life together. Then one day a police officer came to my door. My girlfriend, my companion, the person who made my world rock, was just killed in a car accident. I had just felt my world cave in.

I began to doubt my existence. Was this God's punishment for me being a lesbian? I stayed depressed, searching for answers, I turned to drugs. I ended up losing my job, losing our apartment, and everything I had worked hard to get, was now lost to drugs and misery. Struggling just to eat, I made a mistake that would haunt me for decades to come. I went back to my parent's home and begged for help. My parents took me in and told me of a "wonderful place" I could go and find answers. It was a farm, part of a church organization, where I could work, get close to God, ride horses, and enjoy being around others my age seeking answers.

I left the next day on a plane to Jubilee Home, in Corpus Christi, Texas. I was hoping I could find hope, and what I found instead was pain, anguish and abuse beyond comprehension. The first day I got there, I was informed that my clothes were too "boyish" and that I was to remain looking at the floor at all times until I denounced my horrific desire for women. I was informed, "Homosexuality was a very bad sin and Christians are not homosexual, they go to hell." I must repent and asked to be saved. Immediately I demanded to go back home, and asked for someone to take me back to the airport. I was then informed that I could not leave, even though I was an adult. I was being held there against my will because I was so lost and bad I had to have them reform me to be a good Christian and see the error of my ways.

I started heading towards the door, and when I reached it, I tried to open it, just to find it locked with a key deadbolt. I turned around and told my captors, "This is illegal and you cannot hold me here against my will". I was informed that they do not answer to mans law, but to God's law and I would obey their instruction because they were messengers of God. I knew then I was stuck there until I conformed. Where else would I go?

Day in and day out I worked hard to find myself, find understanding and learn to conform. It was hard. Each night when I went to sleep I cried, hoping that I would either die or wake up from this terrible nightmare. Neither one happened. One day I met a nice friend named Dawn, who I befriended. She had been through many different homes and helped encourage me a lot. She told me the best way to get out of here is play their game, learn what is expected of me, and eventually they will "think" I am converted and it will get easier. She told me about the bad things that would happen if I did not follow all their rules. I tried my best to follow like she did, and we would secretly talk about our true feelings when no one is around.

I lasted a whole 11 months at the home, often isolated in a small closet like room for a few days at a time when I messed up. I learned to pray to a God that I felt had abandoned me, and doomed me to this nightmare. I learned to sing hymns, and quote Bible verses, that bore no meaning because deep inside, I was still bitter. I learned to close my eyes to seeing girls repeatedly abused like in a torture camp. I tried to ignore the sounds of a few girls crying themselves to sleep after being sexually violated by people that were supposed to be men of God. I worked in the kitchen cooking for people I did not like, doing chores and scrubbing floors until my hands ached, chapped and bled. The only thing I did get was to finish high school, in a small classroom. I even got a diploma, that I would find out later was as worthless as the parchment it was printed on.

I got called to the office one day and was told to pack my things. My father had died of cancer, and they were sending me home to help my mother continue to run his small business. I packed immediately, and was taken on a plane home. I lasted a few years helping my mother and brother, all the while hiding who I truly was inside. I went to church on Sundays, and during the week pretended to be the model Christian. All false things must come to an end. I decided to get a job elsewhere and try to be who I was hiding behind my family's beliefs, and a lifestyle I hated.

It has been almost 20 years since I went to Jubilee home. I have never forgotten the things that I experienced, saw and heard. But I have learned that evil does exist. I searched for over 15 years and finally reconnected with my friend Dawn, who helped me through some trying moments. She has been an inspiration to me now and we share so many laughs and tears. We have both moved on.

I now live in Thunder Bay, Ontario. I had to move away to get away from my family and their stalking and harassment. I have a wonderful woman by my side. I do go to Sunday School with my life partner, and we do believe in God. But we believe God loves everyone, and that we should leave the judging of our actions to him. Life has been good to us, and we adopted our son last month.

Jubilee Home, Corpus Christi

Without the support and love of friends, I would not be where I am today, and as my friend reminded me last week, we are "survivors" and no longer "victims". The nightmares have decreased and I am learning to cope much better. I still am very afraid to confront my family because the last time I did, the threats were very real, and I still fear retribution for exposing the truth about Jubilee home. One day I hope I can return to the United States safely, and without fear of harm from my family for going against the Fundamentalist Baptist Church beliefs they cling to.

4~JAMES-LIGHTHOUSE HOME FOR MEN
1982

It was a cold December morning in 1981, when my parents had reached their limit. My dad no longer able to deal with my rebellion against the church and his rules, and decided I was in need of strict discipline and reform. He drove all through the night with me, even brought my uncle along to make sure I did not jump out of the back seat of the car while going down the highway. My uncle was about a foot taller than me and twice my weight, so there was no use in trying anything to escape.

I figured it would be like the boarding schools you hear about where people ride horses, go on campouts, and participate in sports and all the cool stuff, so I might be able to handle it. Besides, no one could be as strict as my dad and the old church we attended back in Ohio.

Let me go back a bit and tell you about my younger years and reflect on what led me to be such an unrighteous sinner that needed reform in the first place. Granted I was a rebel at heart, broke a few small rules, skipped school two times and snuck out of my bedroom window to sit at the park and kiss a girl while watching stars, but I was no criminal by anyone's standards, well at least anyone that was normal.

I had only tried pot once, but my dad did not know. I never stole from stores, had any trouble with the police or had bad grades, so what made me such a bad kid that I had to be sent away? Well according to my father, a deacon at the local bible thumping, pulpit beating fundamentalist church we attended, I was worst of the worst! I was lost and need of salvation and guidance before I became a murderer or some horrible criminal in prison. How he drew that conclusion, I am not sure, but I was after all only 17, and entitled to a few mistakes.

Anyway, there I was, December 22, 1981, in Corpus Christi, Texas, and about to experience what it was like to live in a hell on earth, that no one should have to endure as a kid, no matter how bad their parents think they are.

The very first thing I remember was my dad hugging me and telling me that this was best for me, and he went into an office with another man I learned later was named Brother Crummey. Another man by the name of Brother Mark grabbed my suitcase and escorted me in another direction, informing me en-route that he would have to search my belongings and make sure I had no drugs or alcohol. I told him I had neither because I didn't drink or do drugs, he said I was a liar, because I wouldn't be at the Lighthouse if I were not an addict. Panicked, I stood there wondering what in the world my father had told them to get me into this place.

Brother Mark dumped my clothes on the floor then proceeded to pick thru and then threw away several tee shirts he said were unacceptable, and told me to pick up the rest of my clothes and told me to follow him. I was taken into the dorm and read the rules. I thought home was strict, this was truly hell! I saw small clips about prison systems on television when at some friends houses, but it didn't appear as bad as this place. I am sure it didn't smell as bad either. Pine-sol and sweat was the room deodorizer scent of the week. I was strong enough to make you get a lump in your throat and puke.

No television, no radio, no comic books, no singing any songs except the ones in a church hymnal or the ones they created out of Bible verses. The first week I was assigned a "buddy" who was to follow me everywhere and he even stood in the bathroom when I showered or took a leak.

I was disgusted with the lack of privacy and violation I felt, so I made it appoint to try and not have to use the bathroom during the allowed times he had to go. Sometimes that became quite painful since we had designated times we were allowed to go to the bathroom. You didn't dare ask to go at any random time, or you would be severely punished as I learned quickly.

The first week I was there, the change in diet was so drastic from nutritional meals my mom fixed to home grown flavorless crap sweetened with honey and I ended up with bowels that would scream for relief. It was either ask to go to the bathroom and deal with licks (spanking until our butts swelled) or crap my pants. I just took the beatings and went after seeing what they did to one kid who couldn't hold it, and wet his pants. He couldn't sit for two days.

Lighthouse was full of grown men who had been addicts and alcoholics who were recovering, so I can see where this place might have been what they felt was needed to stop their addiction, but for me a 17 year old who was just being a typical teenager, this was no place to be.

I learned how to pretend to be ashamed of my past, and confessed my alleged sins long enough for my parents to run out of money and get sent home in 6 months. I can thank the home for the wonderful lessons I learned while there.

I learned how have a heart filled with hatred and spite towards a whole lot of people. I learned what it was like to watch grown men have sex in a corner of a pantry when they think no one is looking, and then later preach how much an abomination sex outside of marriage was, and sex with another person of the same sex and homosexuality would lead them to hell.

I learned how humiliating it was to have to pee and have someone get a hard on watching me. I learned how it felt to have food shoved down my throat that I didn't like even when I choked until I threw up, only to be beaten with a board if I puked and then have to clean it up after the beatings. I learned how painful it was to kneel in prayer for hours on end until my knees swelled and I could barely stand.

I learned what it was like to work like a slave out in bean fields from sun up until sundown with very little food, warm dirty water to drink and blisters on my hands for no pay. I learned to hate most religions, and people who preached about self-sacrifice to a God that let me endure six months of a living hell.

Over twenty years have gone by and I finally have worked through some of the issues I had dealing with the home. I left my father's house at 18, and finished my GED in 1984 after spending two years living in and out of shelters and on the street. I had little to no self esteem, spent years living with ups and downs, failures and half finished careers until I went through counseling and came to terms with understanding that the brainwashing they did to me was what was wrong, not me. It is hard to get the sermons out of your head, and lose the sense of worthlessness that they imbed into your brain in such a short time. You become dysfunctional, insecure, angry and hopeless.

I am now a successful store manager and in college studying engineering and met a wonderful woman that I plan to marry soon. She is very supportive and has taught me that I can have faith, I can have love and acceptance by a loving God and faith does not have to include abuse.

I will never forget what I experienced, because I did survive it and seek help, but I fear if society allows these places to continue to abuse and molest people in the name of religion, people are going to get to the point that suicide may be their only option. I can recall there were several occasions when I felt that was the route I would take but chose not to because I actually had friends to intervene and get me the help I needed.

Lighthouse shoreline working cabin

Brother Crummey-The dictator

5~KIM – REBEKAH HOME FOR GIRLS
198X

My name is Kim and I am a 45 year old single mother of two boys. I am struggling though college and just getting back on my feet after a long divorce and years of abuse, failures and depression. I finally started feeling good about myself after two years of counseling and coming to terms with my past and the horrible experiences I endured in foster care from age 5 until I turned 13. I was placed in foster care when my mother overdosed on heroine and they had no idea where any of my other family was. When I heard I was going to be adopted, I thought things would be wonderful and someone would finally love me. I was wrong.

They really did not want me and reminded me often of that. I was expected to clean up after them and their 2 children. I was told repeatedly that I was adopted to help them and should be thankful that I was not in an orphanage. I had to make their beds and mine every morning before school, and manage to keep my grades up to their standard in this school we went to that was part of the church we had to attend.

I had never seen a school like this. They would paddle you if you did not do your homework, and if you had a grade that was below a C, they would paddle you more and make you write sentences or write your homework out two or three times. I always managed to not be good enough, so even after getting paddled in school, I was again paddled at home by my adoptive parents for being an embarrassment to them. I tried running away several times and did not succeed, and finally my foster dad said to me that I was not worth the money they paid him every month for adopting me, and I would have to go with him to a meeting with the pastor of the church who knew of a place to send kids who could not be good Christian soldiers.

We met with the pastor, and I still have not forgotten his description of Rebekah Home for Girls. Gee was he deluded. He said there were horses, and fishing and sports and activities. I would get to enjoy being around girls my age in a dorm setting and learn about farm life, and animals. I would have church services and learn to cook, but most of all I would be away from worldly temptations. This didn't sound bad and I could handle that, if only it were the truth.

I went home with my dad and packed my things, he said we were leaving the next day. I wanted to go back to school and say good-bye to my friends, and he said no, I was not allowed to talk to anyone. I was disheartened, but finished packing a few clothes and a few pieces of jewelry and my favorite stuffed bear I had since my first foster home when I was in kindergarten. I sat quietly that night at the dinner table, nervous and a little bit scared. Once again I was being shuffled to some place where I would not know anyone. I should have been used to that by then since I spent so many years being tossed in and out of foster homes, but I had been here with my adoptive parents over a year, and I had grown attached to some of my friends.

We flew to Texas and at the airport we were met by a nice looking lady with a smile, her husband and some other man, and escorted to a van, and driven quite a distance away. I fell asleep in the van while my father was busy discussing fee arrangements and how lengthy my stay would be. I abruptly woke up when I heard someone say, the average stay is a minimum of one year. I thought to myself, a whole year!! OH no, I would not be home for my old school's Junior/Senior social. Even though we did not dance or party at the private Christian school, the social was considered the go-to event of the year. I just couldn't miss it.

We pulled into the parking lot of what appeared to be a community all on its own. There was a shack like building at the entrance that resembled a guard shack and a man standing at the door of it, that waved us in. We pulled up in front of a large building that had the name on top of the front that said, Rebekah Home for Girls, in red letters on white brick. I got a really sick feeling in my stomach, and started to cry.

Rebekah Home for Girls

I was told I had to say good-bye to my dad and was escorted down a hallway and to a room and told to strip down to my underclothes so I could be checked to make sure I had not snuck anything I was not supposed to have with me. I did. They had me wait in the bathroom and a girl explained to me she was a "helper" and that the other girl was a "Buddy" that would stay with me for a week or two wherever I went until I learned the rules. The "helper" was going to get me a uniform to wear because during school hours, it was required we wear either red or blue double-knit elastic waist ugly skirts. I asked about my clothes and they said I could only wear what was approved and a staff member had to go through my things and remove what I was not allowed to have.

I soon was dressed in a red plaid shirt and red skirt, knowing I looked terrible and glad none of my friends back home could see me looking so stupid. I was then explained the rules and rushed over to the school to get started. I had attended private schools before, where we had a Christian-centered education and religious teachings but we had regular desks, regular textbooks, and teachers that taught classes, and we switched classes like a typical high school. This classroom was one room, with several dozen cubicles with dividers between them. There wasn't any teacher, just monitors and a person in charge called a supervisor.

I quickly learned no one taught us and we were given workbooks that we took a test when finishing and we were to learn to do the work ourselves. I learned later if you did not understand something, guess, mark it wrong and memorize the answer keys when you graded your own work, because asking for help usually got you looked down upon as an idiot. So the year I was there I didn't learn a damn thing. Later having to repeat the whole tenth grade when I returned home.

I was miserable all the time and cried a lot. The buddy I had told me the best way to learn to adjust was either to learn to follow all the rules and comply or get into a lot of trouble and have to go to the lockup room. I heard horror stories of the lockup room, but luckily never saw it. I did see the girls that came out of them after staying in it for weeks on end. They smelled real bad and looked like they had lived in a drainage ditch for two weeks or more. They looked like they had not eaten at all. I tried my best to behave.

Sometimes I had trouble memorizing my Bible verses in time, and it's hard to memorize when you're always doing school work and chores and church. I got marks against me, which led to "licks" which were by no means a lick! They were more like a beating with a board with holes in it that stung like someone had set my butt cheeks on fire. One time when I was getting my licks, I accidentally cussed. Man was I in trouble! I got my mouth washed out with soap and another set of licks until my butt stung tremendously and later when I looked at it I had patches where blood was on my underwear from the rawness. I got stuck back with a buddy for two weeks, and was not allowed to talk to anyone at all except to answer a helper when asked a question. I learned to memorize while taking a shower and brushing my teeth, because I didn't want to experience that often.

During the summer months it was hot and I earned the privilege to work on the farm. I am not sure why it was considered a privilege to milk goats, because they sure stunk. When I was not working on the farm we sometimes got to play kickball or volleyball outside for an hour, but only if we had not gotten into any trouble and no marks all week. A lot of girls did not get to go outside, and I really always wondered what some of the male staff did when they took the girls away, and they always came back crying and shaking.

I did not ask but I had heard rumors that they were being raped to learn submission. I had seen girls get licks so hard they threw up, and then were punched, had their hair pulled and dragged by their hair down the hallway to the lockup room almost weekly. It scared me into being as good as I could no matter how nutty I thought these people were.

Sometimes they had tours of the homes on Sundays, and we got to do activities to appear like we were having fun when visitors were looking, and as soon as they left it was back to the routine. It was like a jail. We had a time for everything, and not much time to do it. We had a specific time to use the bathroom, a limited time to shower and a short time to clean up our rooms. I behaved as best I could, and was so excited when my time was up and I was able to have a visit and my parents took me home. I was there 12 months and 2 days. My parents wanted me to stay longer, but I think they did not have enough money to keep me there. I was just so glad to be going home. Home would be easy to conform to the rules compared to the Rebekah home.

I never spoke of Rebekah home with my parents. I did what I could to readjust, and ended up repeating a grade because I learned nothing at the Rebekah home school. That made my dad mad at them and he seemed to be more caring towards me. I graduated from high school, and went on to college and struggled to adjust. I woke up many times on campus in the dorms with nightmares. Although the college did not have the same rules as Rebekah home, it resembled it with the dorm type arrangements. I ended up quitting and getting a job. I later married, had a son and divorced all within three years.

I spent the next 18 years messing my life up, using drugs, getting clean, and repeating the cycle over and over. I had trouble adjusting to anything that involved someone bossing me around and frequently ducked for cover waiting for someone to grab my hair and drag me around a corner. What was wrong with me? I talked to a coworker and told them about my experience at Rebekah home, and she told me I needed counseling because I was suffering PTSD and that counseling would help me find answers.

I started counseling, and it was hard at first because no counselor believed me, then I took articles I found on the internet about Roloff homes and showed her, and she started understanding. I have been in counseling a few years, and finally got the courage to tell my parents about the harsh abuse I saw happening when I was sent to Rebekah home. They refuse to acknowledge that anything had happened, and that I was a liar as were all the other girls who walked through the doors of that place. I quit trying to defend myself and walked away from my family, hoping one day they will see the truth.

I am now recently remarried with a two year old child and an amazing husband and finally started to work on finishing my college education. The world is getting brighter now that I have learned to get the demons out of my head and filled my heart with all the good in my life. I still think back and wonder how all the other girls are that were there, especially the ones dragged down the hallways by their hair after being beaten, or the girls that were sexually mistreated. I hope they have found the peace within that I have.

Without people understanding how bad it was and believing it exists, abuse will continue. Rebekah home did close physically but all they did was relocate their place of abuse to different states with weaker laws. My goal is to finish college and go to law school and one day work to fight for the rights of kids put into homes that treat kids this way and hold their families accountable for forcing it on them, and the homes for abusing.

Brother & Mrs. Barrett, the dorm Parent of Rebekah

home during my stay.

6~TERRI – REBEKAH HOME FOR GIRLS 1982

Raised a farmer's daughter on a rural Ohio farm, one would think that I would not be easily persuaded by the wiles of the Devil and temptation living three miles from the nearest neighbor and being sent to a church School for my education. But the Devil found and possessed me, if you were to listen to my father describe my behavior to the local pastor of the little Baptist church we attended in town at an after supper meeting he was having in our den with my parents.

I remember my father telling the pastor that he had caught me looking at a boy in the wrong manner and speaking to him without a chaperone at age 15 and this was going to lead me to sin. This happened when I went with him to the hardware store to get some fencing supplies. I thought it quite strange that the boy who held out his hand and helped me up when a man rushing out the hardware store had pummeled me with an 80 lb bag of concrete mix and knocked me to the ground, and I smiled and said "thank you", was something to be considered sinful.

I had never seen that boy since that time and a few months had passed. I continued to listen as my father listed so many more of my sinful ways; I had listened to music that was not about God or the church, I was ungrateful to my parents for being providers because I refused to eat the liver and peas mom made a month ago for Sunday dinner and threw a fit when I was spanked for throwing it in the trash. I was caught dancing and holding my skirt up enough to show my kneecaps and this was a foul showing of my flesh, and I was surely doomed for a life of whoredom for it. I stole another cookie from the cookie jar and was sure to become an armed robber if I continued to do this. He went on for what seemed hours and I had drifted off to sleep on the sofa thinking to myself he had a lot of nerve thinking I was going to turn into a whore, when the awful things he did to me would make any person's skin crawl. One day I was a sinner, and another I was paying penance to him by being his "special princess" and playmate, in a manner that was not proper.

When I woke up about two hours later, I noticed the pastor was leaving out the back door and he gave me a weird look and pointed to me and told me he would see that I would learn to be a woman of God one day, and he knew just the place to see that it happened. That struck fear in me but knew that there was nothing I could do about it because he was a man of God and we were always taught to follow men of God. I could see in the shadows of the back porch light my mother wiping tears from her eyes as she whisked off towards the side of the house.

I was so exhausted that I went upstairs to my room and kicked my shoes off and crawled into bed with my sundress and sweater on, too tired to change into my pajamas, I cried myself to sleep. Before I knew it, the alarm went off and I hopped out of bed to be met by my mother standing next to a suitcase propped on a chair by my dresser. She was pulling some of my clothes from the drawer and quietly placing them in the suitcase and wiping tears from her eyes. I asked her what was going on, and she asked me to hush and understand that my father was the head of the house and the Lord had spoken to him, and I must be sent away to learn God's will and my ungodly ways must be cast from me. Scared of being sent away to a strange place and heartbroken, I went into the bathroom and washed up, changed my clothes and headed out to do my usual morning chores and spend time with my little sister getting our tasks done before we had to rush and get ready to meet the school shuttle van at 7.

My sister and I did our chores. She was 6 years younger than me and usually wanted to play more than work, aggravating me, but this time I was not annoyed, I actually enjoyed it. I had a feeling I would be separated from her and would miss her dearly. I then heard my father come out to the barn and tell me I needed to go into the house and take a bath and change into one of my Sunday dresses because I was going to take a long drive with him to Texas. Afraid of my father's belt, I complied. I came back downstairs dressed in my Sunday best, and went over to hug my mother who was holding my little sister and sobbing. I held onto her as tight as I could when my father grabbed my arm and pulled me away from her, screamed that she was disrespecting his authority and then he slapped my mother so hard she almost fell off the chair. I was so mad I kicked my father's shin and he proceeded to drag me out to the barn for a last lesson in obedience before we got in the truck to leave.

When we got into the barn he pulled off his belt and yelled for me to raise my dress and bend over the bale of hay. I did, and with each swing of the belt, the sting grew unbearable and my anger grew deeper, until I think I passed out. I am not sure what happened right after that, I woke up and I was in the passenger seat of the truck with my suitcase on the floorboard, it was dark out, my butt hurt so bad and so did other unmentionable parts of my anatomy. I looked up at my father and he said we would stop for some food and I could use the bathroom, but if I spoke a word to anyone I would end up dying and going to hell. I was so frightened that I believed him and made sure to look specifically at no one when we did stop and I had to pee.

I got into the gas station bathroom and barely could sit on a toilet, my bottom hurt something awful. I leaned around to look and it was swollen red and purple, and I had blood on my dress from where some sore spots had bled through my underwear and slip. I now understood why I had a very long heavy coat on and it was not very cold out. My dad was hiding the blood stains from other's view, so they would not know he beat me or maybe find out any other dirty secrets of what he did to me. I sure was not going to tell anyone. I was hoping that when I get to this place that I would like it much better than home because my father never mentioned his beatings to the pastor or anyone in the church, so maybe they were not as strict as my father and I would not have to be anyone's "special princess" any more.

We stopped at some rest area and my dad said we would sleep in the truck bed under the camper shell for the night and he ordered me into the back and tied my hands together and tied the rope to a hook like thing on the inside of the back of the camper shell. He said it was for my own good and so I would not run away and be snatched by someone of the Devil. I curled up on some old horse blankets and stared out the back and wondered if there is a God in heaven, and if he is as kind as the Bible says then why won't he let me die and get out of this place? I eventually drifted off to sleep.

We had been on the road now for three days and my father pulled over at a gas station and told me to go change into another dress and throw that one into the trash because we only had a few hours before we arrived at the place I was going to be staying. Then he told me to remember to wash my face and brush my hair so I would be presentable when we arrived. I did so and we were back on the road. Within a few more hours we arrived at Rebekah Home for Girls. We were instructed that it was mealtime so we headed with an escort over to a dining hall with the words "Come and Dine on the side of it, later I would learn it should have read "come eat with swine" since the food was as fitting as slop for hogs, and not humans.

We were greeted by a couple that looked not much older than my parents age, and they both smiled and said that we could sit and eat with them and then they would have a staff member take me over and show me the dorms and my father could go with them to the offices and take care of paperwork. We ate, I tried not to vomit, but it was dry, flavorless, casserole of some sort that tasted like paste and the cooked carrots were cooked so long and mushy they were almost yellow instead of orange. I asked if I could pass on finishing because I felt ill from the long drive, and was glad that they accepted the explanation and allowed me to skip eating the gross stuff they called lunch.

I was asked to follow this older lady and another girl a little bit older than me, to the dorm. I got up and walked with them. The girl seemed really nice but the older lady seemed quite mean, and when she looked away the girl that was with us made faces at her, which made me smile a little. The older lady turned and saw me smiling and became angry and told me I must not smile at the other girl. She was on "silence" punishment and her "helper" was on a visit with her parents, so she was not to be spoken to. She turned back around and was looking at someone down a hall, and the girl looked at me and we smiled and both stuck our tongues out at the lady when she wasn't looking.

Of course at age 15 it may have been immature to do, but it sure was fun at the moment. That is until she turned around and caught us. The look on her face convinced me I was really in deep trouble now. She sternly told me to sit on a chair and wait, then led the other girl by the arm down a hall and into a room and slammed the door behind her. I heard some yelling, then some spanking, and crying. I sat there near shaking and afraid I was going to be spanked next and my butt was already so sore and bruised from my father's beatings. I thought if I had another spanking I would probably die.

The lady came back out and then told me my behavior was not tolerable and she would let it slide that time, I sighed and apologized and she told me her name was Mrs. Barret and she was the dorm mother and she would show me to my room where I would shower and be searched and assigned a helper, and told the rules of the dorm. I quietly followed her as we passed down a long hall with a lot of doors to bedrooms. We got to one that had three beds in it and a bathroom that was attached to another bedroom with three more beds. She said this would be my room and that she would explain some of the rules to me while we waited for the girl who was to be my "helper" came back from lunch.

I was given the rules, and there were not too many that were different than the rules at home, except the ones about memorizing Bible verses and praying a lot. That was a lot more than we did at home, but it felt like it was going to be much better to pray and memorize scriptures than be around my dad who made me feel dirty and nasty inside. I thought to myself this would be easy to do. I was happy to be here and away from my father because this lady seemed nice. I was very naive and learned really quickly that trusting this lady was not a good idea.

The first few weeks it was hard to learn all the rules and I got demerits often, several "licks" as they called the paddling's, and was put on silence for a week once for spitting at someone who made fun of my curly hair that was always getting tangled when we did chores. I tried really hard to go by the rules, and did well enough that within 4 months I was made a helper and found myself in charge of the girl who had stuck her tongue out at Mrs. Barret a few months ago with me. Her name was Lisa, and we became good friends and I explained to her that all she had to do was pretend she loved the place, and pretend to praise God and try hard to follow the rules and maybe one day we both would escape this crazy place. She and I made a pact to follow the rules real good and I would try to look out for her. She eventually made helper too and we both learned to play the "Christian" role so well, that we got to go for walks on the ministry compound grounds on Sunday afternoons without supervision. We were so compliant that they were not afraid we would run away, and we were too afraid to for fear someone would do some of the horrible things we heard rumors of.

I was there a whole year, and was eventually allowed to go home. Upon my return home, I learned my father had been ill and had a stroke. God is a good God after all, because now he couldn't put his filthy hands on me, he was in a nursing home, and it was just my mother and sister at the farm. I was so happy to be with my mom and sister that I never spoke much of the Rebekah Home and just cherished my family and the freedom.

I was never tossed into any of the confinement rooms at Rebekah Home, but saw many of the girls who refused to follow the rules wind up in them for days and sometimes weeks at a time. You could sneak past the doors and hear them crying inside and the echoes of preaching and prayer blaring from the speakers inside the room 24 hours a day. I felt bad for them, but any showing of sympathy would have put me into one of the rooms also.

I watched girls who were favorites of some of the male staff go different places on the ministry property alone and come back with looks of disgust on their faces and the men usually wearing snide grins on their faces and after asking one time, and learning of the rapes, I kept silent for fear of it happening to me again like my father had done so many times, telling me a woman must always learn to submit to a man of authority without question. I was really happy that I was never chosen by one of the male staff to ever be a part of that. The licks and other punishments of washing dishes in mass quantities over and over again then mopping floors until you could eat off of them was enough for me.

I graduated high school when I was 19 because I had to repeat the whole year of high school, since Rebekah Home had a school that was not accepted by my local school and was not accredited. I went on to college and struggled to deal with who I was and what my beliefs were going to be based on. I went to church in a different town than when I grew up. It was not as strict as the church I went to as a kid, but they still preached the gospel and were loyal to the fundamentalist Baptist movement, and supported the Roloff Ministries and Rebekah Homes, and other homes like them. I ended up leaving that church and not going at all to a Baptist church ever again. I married my husband in 1997 and we started a family.

Things went well until after our third child. I started experiencing nightmares and battled depression. My husband suggested I get counseling and he would go with me. We did and I started sharing the stories of my past.

My husband believed me, but the counselors thought I was crazy and imagined it all and suggested that I be hospitalized or medicated. My husband suggested we do neither and seek out a better counselor. I spent a few years looking and nearly drank myself to sleep every night in the process. It took a toll on our family and my husband, but he stood by me the whole time.

In 2005 I found an AOL chat website where another girl from Rebekah Home had posted about her abuse, and we became friends. We shared many good and bad memories and she told me about a group of counselors near where I currently lived that work with people that have been survivors of religious cults like what we experienced.

I am doing great, and I still keep in touch with my friend, and have found so many new sites about institutions people have been in like the one I was in and have reconnected with a few survivors. I have still been a bit nervous and scared as some of the survivor groups had people I knew were still supporters of the prisons, yet acted like survivors, so I pretty much stay to myself and my few friends in Missouri.

My husband and I are doing wonderful in our remodeling business and have been blessed with a healthy family. I am glad I was able to move on, but am disheartened that no matter how much people fight to expose these places of torture in the name of God, they still exist; beating, raping and brainwashing boys and girls into submission. They must be stopped. Telling our stories can help, that is why I am telling mine.

The Rebekah Home girls

7~KAREN – JUBILEE HOME FOR WOMEN 1983

In the fall of 1982 I was a typical mother of a beautiful new infant daughter and a wonderful husband who was an associate pastor at our local church that I grew up in. We were Baptist, but not Fundamentalists. I grew up in the church, but it was not as strict as most churches are. My husband worked during the week at a local electronics store and I taught at the preschool up until our daughter was born. Life seemed good. We were a new family, and had a decent income and a new home. I was looking forward to being a mom and spending time watching our family grow and do things together.

Christmas had come and went. My husband and I were planning a small get together at our home for a few friends. Games and watching the ball drop in Time Square was our intent for New Years Eve, but those plans failed when I went to check on my daughter who had been sleeping past her normal feeding time and I grew concerned. I went into her crib and saw her lifeless pale blue body, and screamed for my husband. I picked her up and tried to do CPR while he called the local emergency number to get an ambulance. They arrived within minutes and resumed the CPR I had started as they rushed her to the hospital.

My husband and I followed behind them in the car, panic stricken we ran a few stop signs and lights trying to stay with the ambulance as best we could. When we arrived at the hospital we were rushed aside to fill out paperwork and speak with a nurse as our little bundle of joy was rushed lifelessly on a stretcher loaded with equipment into a room behind double doors. We were within minutes greeted by a physician and a hospital chaplain and ushered down a hall towards a room. I was confused as to why they were not taking us to see our beautiful angel. I learned why as soon as the door closed. The doctor said there was nothing they could do, it was a rare heart defect, and her heart had a valve that ruptured and she had gone to heaven. My world then fell apart.

We spent a few days with my daughter's funeral and time with family. I spent my time being angry with God for taking my baby away from me. I couldn't find any peace or comfort in my husband's words or the encouragement from others that it will get easier over time. Who were they to tell me how to feel? Over the next several months I started drinking heavily to forget the pain. My husband and I started growing apart. I loved him very much and did not want to lose the one thing that mattered to me that I loved and still had. He told me I needed to get help for the drinking and get myself back on track, but we were not sure where to turn. So we talked to the pastor of our church.

He told us he had heard from another pastor about a place that was full of Christian love and I could get the help that was needed, and since we did not have a lot of money after borrowing to pay for my daughter's funeral, this place would allow me to work on the grounds to pay for my boarding. This sounded wonderful and I could find answers for the pain in my life and get back to not being angry at God and find peace once again in my life. I wanted to do anything I could to save my marriage, and begin again with the love of my life. I packed my bags and was on a flight to the Jubilee Home for women within a week of calling them.

When I first arrived, the adjustment was hard. The rules were much stricter than I was accustomed to at our church back home. The NKJV version of the Bible I had was considered a mockery and they took that from me and gave me someone's tattered and worn out King James Version Bible and then they proceeded to take the majority of my clothes away from me because they were too "spirited and bright colors and might attract other men at the facility and that would make me a harlot. I asked to call my husband to see if he could mail me some of my other clothes, being they took so many of mine away, and they told me "no". I was not allowed to call home for the first month, because it might lead me to not focus on God and my recovery. They had a clothing closet and I could pick from their approved attire that was available, which consisted of tattered, worn and stained crap that looked like it belonged in rag boxes for cleaning, but I would have to make do.

I spent the first week in my room in tears, asking God why it was so difficult to not be angry at him, and why I felt so out of place here. I knew I loved God and the Bible teachings I had grown to love since I was a toddler, but here, this place, did not feel like it was a place of love. Something just did not seem right. I was a "Newbie" so I had someone that followed me everywhere I went, to make sure that I, a grown adult, was not tempted by the Devil, and flee the facility. I did not like this idea. I was a grown woman and who was to tell me I was not allowed to leave a place that was not jail, and I was not sentenced by a court to be there?

I knew that after 30 days I could call my husband and tell him that I needed him to come and get me as soon as possible, this was not a place I wanted to be. The first three weeks went by slower than I had ever experienced. Here I was in my early 20's held captive in a Church-based concentration camp. I did my best to follow the rules and memorize the scriptures and pray. I knew that if I silently prayed to the God I grew up loving, that he would hear my prayers. I still could not understand how these women could all be here on their own volition and willing to experience these harsh conditions voluntarily.

We would get up very early in the morning and clean our rooms, read scriptures and pray, then head over to the kitchens to start cooking. We did not only cook for our home, but for the Rebekah girls home and staff from all over the farm facility. We were to follow this strict schedule and if we compromised anything or went off task or took a break without permission, or even went to the restroom outside of a designated time, we were considered being sinful and not committed to God's will and punished. I was 23 years old and how dare anyone try and punish me like this! I demanded to call my husband or the police. They said I have let the devil get a hold of me and needed some isolation time to get my heart right. I was abruptly escorted to a closet like room and shoved into it, and handed my Bible as the door closed behind me. There was a mattress on the floor and a bucket in a corner with a lid and a roll of toilet paper resting atop of it. I thought to myself, you have got to be kidding!

I spent two or three days in that closet. I am not sure why they gave me my Bible as there was not enough ample lighting to read. Just me, 4 very dark walls, a bucket for a toilet, an occasional meal tossed in the door by someone who was reminding me they were praying for my soul, and that speaker hanging from the ceiling that pumped in preaching and prayer 24/7. I felt like this was Bible-Hell. What in the world had I gotten myself into?

Was I ever going to get out of this place?   Did my husband even know how bad this place really was? Is this what I get for being mad at God for taking my daughter from me as an infant?   So many questions, and feeling hopeless, that I collapsed on the floor and cried for almost the last day and a half I was in that closet, so-called the Redemption Room, on the Hall of Prayer.

I prayed to God that if he let me out of there, I would do his will and follow the scriptures and be a good Christian wife. I was let out within a few days and the staff asked me had I gotten myself right with God, and I said yes I had made my peace with God. I spent the next several days being as compliant as I could, knowing I would get to speak with my husband in a few more days, and he would come and rescue me. I just had to hold out as best I could until then.

I finally got to make my one phone call. My husband was on the other end, and I cried so hard and talked so fast. I begged him to come and get me, this place was crazy and I was locked in a closet, he said to me he would be on the road in a few hours to get me. The staff who had listened in on my conversation became very angry with me and voiced it. They told me I did not appreciate them trying to help me get my life right with God. I needed to understand that God took my baby from me because I was not a good enough Christian to deserve a child. That just tore me to pieces inside, and I was bitter at these people who tried to blame me for losing my child. They isolated me in a room by myself, which had its own bathroom and I was to stay there until my husband came and got me.

My husband came and picked me up. I was so happy to see him and knowing that I was leaving this place was even better. We drove outside the property and he pulled over to the side of the road and apologized for what he had allowed me to go through and we cried together, holding each other, and swore that we would put this behind us and move forward. We drove home. We grew closer together and have since had two beautiful boys that grew up knowing we love them and never spoke of the place again until we saw stories on the news about religious homes and the abusive tactics used on teenagers. My husband looked at me and started asking questions about what happened to me. I told him all about the Jubilee Home and he held me close and told me that we needed to get a hold of someone and tell them what we know about these places and make an effort to stop the abuse and shut them down.

I began to surf the internet and found a few support groups and found someone looking to share the survivor stories of people who had been in any of the Roloff Homes. I started emailing her and we became friends again after I realized I knew her from the Jubilee Home and she was one of the nicest people I knew there but one who was always defiant and winding up in the Redemption room. I think she was there about 3 of the 5 weeks I was at the place. I shared with her many tears and laughter and our experiences after leaving that place. We talked about different staff people we both knew and then sighed in relief. We were survivors of the billion dollar business of human trafficking and abuse in the name of the Independent Fundamentalist Baptist cult.

Jubilee Home girls Spring of 1983

8~MARK – LIGHTHOUSE HOME FOR YOUNG MEN 1974

A rebel with no hope is what everyone considered me in 1981. I was an alcoholic by age 13 and heavy into drugs by 15. No matter what my parents tried to do, I had a mind of my own and was not willing to abide by anyone's rules. I stole car radios to pay for drugs and swiped any alcohol I could from stores and ran the streets at night. In and out of the juvenile system and with no hope, the state of Texas gave my parents a choice. Find a place to send me or I would have to spend the next two or more years in a juvenile work farm.

My father was not too fond of the local judicial system, being he was a cop at one time and was fired because of my conduct. So he was on a mission to find the first place available to send me. I was about to turn 16 so the options were slim on places I could go. He found a Place called Anchor Home for Boys, but they were full and since I was close enough to 18 and an addict they said I would be better off fighting my addiction and getting on the right road to recovery at the Lighthouse Home for Young Men. So the next day we were on the road to the beginning of my living hell and years of recovery from the abuse that would encompass my stay.

There are not many things I can say about the place that would give light to the true picture of the hell I experienced, and the only thing I took away from there was the fact they did clean the drugs out of my system, but not without a price. A price I would pay for years to follow. We were isolated from any normal civilization. The compound was self contained for the most part and any resources needed off the compound were brought in on trucks by outsiders. We ate some of the most disgusting food, except the fish we caught during the week from the inter-coastal waterway, that was deep friend and we ate every Sunday. Although after over two years of having it every Sunday, I don't really care for speckled brown trout any more, let alone any fish substance for that matter.

There was no access to any televisions, radio or newspapers, so the only thing we knew or heard about the outside world was what was hand fed us by the staff of the homes. The rules were worse than any juvenile center I had been to, and could not understand how they managed to survive staying open, and learned later it was politically backed by people with power and financial contributions from the Fundamentalist movement. Money will make people stay silent.

I spent two years being beaten often, forced to kneel on 2 x 4 boards with a bible held over my head until the pain reeled from my knees and I fainted. I was locked in isolation rooms for weeks at a time, deprived of a shower, and proper toilet facilities, and forced to be exposed to preaching, singing and prayers over a loud speaker round the clock while in isolation, in an attempt to brainwash me into conformity. I knew the only way to survive and get out of this place was to submit to their teachings, accept their faith, be sodomized often by a 30 some year old staff member, and accept this as my reality until I left.

Two years and four months later I left the Lighthouse, nearly brainwashed that I was an unworthy piece of crap that nobody would want. But they could not keep me any longer. I was a legal adult and free to go. I left and headed down the road, and hitchhiked to Oklahoma. I was so confused as to my identity, what was right or wrong to believe, that I couldn't function. My father would not let me come home, because I had left the home before the staff felt I was reformed enough. And he was afraid I would embarrass him in the community. I lived on the streets and in a men's shelter in Houston, Texas.

I spent time in and out of jail and between odd jobs and shelters drinking myself near to death until I finally got myself cleaned up thanks to the Salvation Army and a program they had for alcoholics with no hope. I came to terms with my failings and started to see a light at the end of my dismal tunnel of life. I entered a GED program because I found out the High School diploma I received at the Lighthouse was not accepted as a credentialed high school. I wanted to go to college, and finally enrolled in 1998. I graduated in 2002 and married my beautiful wife and we had twins in June of 2004. I never really spoke much of the Lighthouse, and although we both go to church, we practice the Catholic faith which makes us happy with ourselves and is filled with understanding and love.

My father passed away from Lung Cancer in 2006, but I did spend time with him before his death, and we mended our broken fences and I told him the story of my life at the Lighthouse. He believed me and apologized for the many lost years we had. I forgave him for sending me there, and he forgave me for all the things I did that were awful and led me to wind up there. I have found peace in God and my new life. There is healing after this type of abuse, but it is a long road. I hope by telling my story, I can help people who have experienced abuse in any institution to come forward and tell their story. Fight legislature to make changes in the laws that allow this kind of abuse to be shoves under the carpet. We can all work together to shut the places down. I intend to do what I can from where I live here in Ontario. Yes Canada has it's abusive places too.

Forced to pose with our Bibles, we were "Soldiers in God's Army and they were our swords"

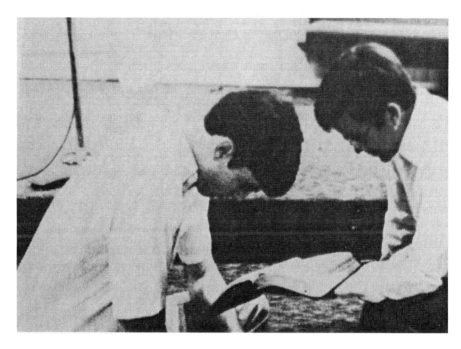

The only way to seek freedom from the abuse was to repent and ask for mercy repeatedly until we were brainwashed to conform.

9~JOHN – ANCHOR HOME FOR BOYS 1979

My name is John and I am a survivor of the Anchor Home for Boys, or as we referred to it, Anchortraz, since it might as well have been in the category of prisons, and it felt as horrific as one. A juvenile detention facility would have been better than my experiences there from 1979-80. There are really no words to describe the feeling when you're there without eliminating the expletives that come to mind as I recall the year-long physical torment, verbal abuse and brainwashing I experienced as a young teenager in the care of the most vile and hateful religious people I have ever encountered in my lifetime.

I never really could understand how a boy of 14 could be so bad to wind up in a facility so twisted in ideologies that they felt the need to force their Fundamentalist ideals on us in such a manner that as an adult, I still cannot even stomach stepping foot into a church to this day. I know and believe that God exists, yet every time I come near a church, I have flashbacks to the days when we were beaten into submission and deprived of basic humane conditions, all in attempts to make us, as they put it, "Good Christian Soldiers".

My first few weeks at Anchor home, I had a really hard time adjusting to the conditions of such a strict environment. Although I was raised in a Christian family and home, the rules were not as stringent. There were no televisions anywhere, no radios, and no contact really with the outside world. Our only contact was people in the home or on the premises of the Roloff Ministries compound and Peoples Baptist Church. I am sure this was to guarantee all the dirty little secrets contained there, that they were afraid we might reveal.

The day of my arrival I was placed on watch list and assigned a buddy to make sure I did not run away, and they were to help me learn the rules and adjust. Not that it would do any good, since the first day I tried like hell to run away and found myself experiencing the embracing warmth of a wooden board meeting my ass cheeks quite hard in rapid succession until my flesh was seared from the lashes and I wished I had been dead. Then I was thrown into a small room with a mattress on the floor and a toilet and nothing more. I was told I was going to stay there until I realized I was here until I found God in my life and was saved. I remember thinking to myself, saved from what? Who was going to save me from them?

I spent a few days in that awful room, and tried to think of ways to escape the next chance I could, but it was hard to process any thoughts with preaching by their fearless leader Lester Roloff, being pumped over a loudspeaker attached to the ceiling of the room twenty-four hours a day on a loop and repeating the sermons and songs hourly. I wanted to rip what little bit of hair I had left out, but it was too hard to grab stubble since they shaved me near bald right after they strip searched and fondled me within an hour of my arrival to that place.

When I was allowed out, I was told that I needed to follow all the rules and until I learned to give myself to God, I would never be able to survive.

Eventually after a few months of repeat beatings, a few more times of being forced to skip a meal, choked and spit on, and shoved in that confinement room, I finally figured out the way to survive was just to comply and submit to their demands. So I started memorizing the Bible verses, started learning the church songs, started learning how to pretend I was praying, until I started believing some of the garbage they were forcing on me. I did so well that one of the workers pulled me aside and told me he could tell that I had Jesus in my heart, because I was not the same kid that he knew a few months prior.

I kept working real hard to always comply, and do what was expected. After four months I was made a helper and watcher of other new boys that came in to the home. I was like a mentor to help teach them the rules. Holy bat poop, I had been brainwashed! Well not exactly, part of me still had a hate for the place and I knew this was what I had to do to survive. I made it another month and was going great in school, good in the dorm, had memorized my scriptures well, started singing in the boys choir group and becoming the perfect example of what forced submission demanded of me. So well in fact, that I started being taken out of the home and to the country store for some ice cream and special errands with a staff member.

Then the weekend came, that would alter my life forever. I was told that since I was doing so well, I was going to be allowed to go to the inter-coastal waterway, to a cabin on the water and go fishing with some staff from the home and with some people from the older guys home called Lighthouse, and we could cook out on a grill and play Frisbee in the sand. I was so excited I could hardly wait for Friday to get here. Friday came and I packed a change of clothes in a drawstring laundry type bag they gave me, and went with a staff member out to a van and we were off headed down the road. This was the first time I had been off the property anywhere in 8 months. I was watching all the cars go by and almost forgot what traffic looked like.

We arrived a little while later at what looked like a fishing shack on the water way. We went inside and the staff member unloaded gas cans from the van and said he was going to start the generator for power and we could start fishing shortly and the others that were meeting us would arrive soon. He said I could walk around, but not wander far because of wildlife and snakes. I was not from Texas, so I was not sure what type of wild creatures he meant so I stayed very close to the cabin. He finished getting the power on and we headed down the docks with the fishing poles that were in the cabin and began to fish.

It was hot and I started to sweat, he said if I got too hot I could just take of my clothes and swim in my underwear since I had no swimming trunks and there were no girls around. I had swam in my underwear before back home in Kansas with my friends when we used to sneak down to the creek after school, so I thought nothing of it, and stripped my clothes off and jumped right in. The water felt so good. I swam around for a few minutes then got out of the water and sat back down on the dock. The staff member told me, I should go in the cabin and change, and he would start fixing us something to eat, since the others had not arrived yet and he thought they might be running late and we should eat before it got dark. I got up and headed into the cabin to get dry underwear on and redressed.

While in the cabin I noticed an old cassette player with a tape in it. I clicked it on and it started playing songs from church we knew, so I decided to sing along to pass the time as I changed, unaware at the time, until I turned around that the staff member had entered and stripped down naked and was touching himself staring at me. I backed up into the corner of the room, scanning my eyes all around searching for something I could grab and hit him with it if he came near me. There was nothing. I ran around the room yelling and then told him that the others might get here and catch him, and that if he touched me I was going to tell on him. He said there were no other people coming, and no one would believe me if I told. I panicked, and he came after me.

I had never in my life imagined such horror until that man started touching me, kissing me and then he grabbed me by my head and shoved my face into his groin and demanded I "service him". He said if I didn't then he would beat me and tell them I tried to run away. I had no clue what in the world he met, but he was all too willing to force instruction on me. I did what I had to do, and then spent the next several hours sitting on the dock naked and vomiting into the water. I felt so gross I wanted to just drown myself. I was helpless. He came and sat by me and told me now that I was his special kid, I will have special privileges and if I ever told anyone, I would spend the rest of my time in the confinement room and he would make sure I never got to see my parents or go home until I was 18.

It was nighttime and we went to sleep in the cabin. I lay there half the night unable to sleep, and wondering if I was going to burn in hell. Lester Roloff had preached many times from the pulpit that men that lay with men and women who lay with women will have their place in hell, so I thought that is where I was going to go. We went back to the anchor home the next day, and he told other staff members I was a great kid and that no fish were biting and that was why we didn't catch anything. I just went to my room and said I was not feeling well from maybe eating something that my stomach didn't agree with. They let me go lay down until evening Bible Study time.

I tried even harder to be the best I could so maybe God would forgive me and I would get to go to heaven since it was not my fault. I never spoke of the incident and it only happened two more times. My parents came to visit and right before I saw them I was reminded that if I ever spoke of anything that happened, I would be forced to stay there longer because they would tell my parents I had done bad things like lying and stealing. I still remained silent. I spent two days with my parents at the visitors place and I talked about how wonderful the place was and how the people had helped me learn about God and how good being a Christian was. My father and mother were very proud and said they were taking me home because they missed me.

I went home with them. I never spoke of what happened. I did well in high school and graduated then went on to college. I was very insecure in relationships and how I felt about myself after the incident at Anchor, and battled depression for years. I started going to counseling, and then finally worked up the courage to tell my parents the truth about Anchor. When I did, they didn't believe me until a few years later when they had heard rumors that the homes were shut down for abuse. They believed physical abuse, but never accepted the sexual abuse to this day. I don't hold it against them though. It is hard to comprehend that grown men posing as Christians would do such a thing, but it happened, and I will never forgive them or forget it.

Cabin outside the dock house at inter-coastal waterway.

10~GREG-STAFF KID ROLOFF MINISTRIES 19XX

I try hard not to remember my teen years at the Roloff homes, the farm and the whole shithole we lived in. Although I was not a resident in the reform homes, but a staff member's kid, I saw far more than I care to remember. We lived in a trailer with no air conditioning just off the airstrip that Lester Roloff used to keep his single-engine Cessna plane.

I remember many a day walking the mile up the road to attend the ACE school that was worthless as far as really educating anyone in any proper fashion if you planned to attend any public colleges. I was determined to attend a state university, so later I had to complete a GED, being the school had zero accreditation, and there was no way I was going to attend a religious college after having so much Jesus already crammed down our throats day in and day out.

When we were not in school, we would be forced to work with other staff members around the farm, either helping milk cows or planting crops and plowing the fields. I may have felt that was harsh working 10 hour days all summer long for no pay, but it was nothing in comparison to what I saw happen to so many of the guys and gals that resided in the group homes.

We were not allowed to talk to any of the girls except for the special ones who had earned the privilege of being considered superior to the others. These I referred to as the ass kissers and suck ups. The ones who were in total compliance and used their status to shove around, call names and assault their fellow dorm mates, just to impress the group home staff. I felt bad for their victims and for them also because they were so brainwashed by these people. I made a comment once to my father and after getting a whipping I wouldn't forget for a long time, I learned to keep my opinions to myself.

I recall one time we were working in the fields digging up carrots and loading them into boxes. There were several boys from the Anchor Home working around us and staff standing there taunting them and kicking dirt in their faces if they were not working fast enough. They would start laughing at them and drinking cold beverages, teasing them and telling them they had to earn their water. It was over 120 degrees in the baking sun and we staff kids all had water, and I tried to share some of mine. One of the Anchor staff members said to me that these boys were worthless trash and I was not to waste my water on them or they would see to it that I was punished harshly by my father. I pretended to feel sick and went home before I lost my temper and hit one of them.

My dad got wind of my attempts to assist the other kids with water, and he warned me that I needed to understand they are being punished for their sins against God and their families and must always listen to the

Anchor staff or find myself there right with them. I was ashamed that my father had become so brainwashed that he believed their crap. I may have been only a teenager, but I had a conscience and knew it was wrong, but who could I call and tell about it? My parents never went into town, there were no phones except in the main staff buildings, and you could not get a phone line to off the compound unless you went through the switchboard in the main offices, and they listened in on the calls. I knew that because my mother worked the switchboards when one of the ladies got sick.

Things always seemed to be changing and tensions were rising with the state. I remember Brother Roloff preaching from the pulpit on Sundays that the government was trying to shut them down for false claims of abuse. I sure wanted to speak up and say, "Well what the hell you call what you're doing?" But I knew my place, and knew I had just a few years left until I would be 18 and leave this place. We were told we had to be on the lookout for any law enforcement sneaking on the property, and if we spoke to them we would be harshly punished by God. Trust me, it takes years to get that fear out of your head when some of the people there would tell us that the reason a family or another staff member was gone overnight it was God's will and they suffered the wrath of God. As a kid I thought they had been struck by some lightning bolt from heaven. That may sound silly, but when you hear it screamed at you from a pulpit almost every Sunday, you start to believe that any time you even think something that does not fit into their plan for you in your service to them; you're doomed to some horrid event or death.

I was always glad when school started back up and we resumed our worthless to the outside world education. It meant no more working around the compound and Friday evenings sitting on a fence post sling-shooting dirt clods at cows, because we were tired of milking them by hand at 4 am. Sometimes we were actually allowed to get on a bus with several staff members to go do things in town, but of course we were watched closely and knew to not breathe a word to the negative to anyone outside of the organization. Guys didn't have it near as bad as the girls. We didn't stand out as much as they did. Girls were only allowed to wear dresses or them culottes that went down past their knees. A fashion nightmare! I felt bad for them because any time we were in town, as rare as it was, they were pointed to and laughed at often.

From all the appearances this was a semi-normal place to those looking in from the outside. We had sports, cheerleaders and activities. But behind the walls of the dorms, the girls had to pay a price. You could hear some of the whispers from them and it would make my skin crawl every time I heard them.   I would see some of the girls that had earned the privilege to participate in the limited activities under watchful eyes of staff, treat the other girls so hatefully, and giggle amongst themselves when they reported a misgiving and a girl was punished. I even heard a few girls one time, brag about how they had done something and blamed someone else they didn't like and that girl was harshly punished. I felt even worse for the girl, because I saw her a week later with bruises all over her one leg and arm and a blackened bruised neck a week later.

That place was far from normal and I will never forget the day we packed up and left there. My dad said he was called to ministry elsewhere, but I heard my parents talking later that night. They were mentioning police and that a raid was about to take place and they didn't want to go to jail. We left there and went to North Carolina, where my dad accepted a job as an associate pastor of a small church. The experience was not anything like the Roloff places, but I was so full of disgust towards God and the faith that I toughed it out long enough to reach 18 and bailed.

I moved on with my life and tried to forget everything I felt and saw, I was still afraid that something might happen to me. I still avoid a church unless someone is getting married or a funeral. I really do not speak to my dad much. My mother on occasion, when I visit her at the mental hospital where she has been since 1995 when she went totally nuts, and never recovered. I can't undo my past; I just know I am making every effort to rewrite my future. I finally quit seeing images of that place in my dreams and nightmares just in the last few years. I saw a survivors' group, and started reading the stories. It reconfirmed exactly what I thought, and I felt bad that I could do nothing to help them, because just like they were isolated, so were we, if not physically, we were emotionally through the brainwashing and imminent fear of harm.

I hope that the survivors of the homes understand that us staff kids had it a lot easier, but we saw their pain and know as they have come forward and started to speak about it, I believe them. I hope they too one day find the healing they need.

Workers who had us pick vegetables for produce companies for no pay, that brought profits into the organization.

The cows I used to sling-shot dirt clods at, they looked pretty skinny.

Ditch digging to fix water/sewer lines usually was done by hand when equipment outdated was never replaced, because they were too cheap to fix stuff.

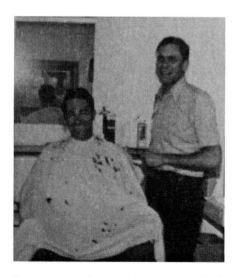

No reason to leave the compound, they even had their own barber so you would be more inclined to stay isolated.

No need to go to a mechanic if you happened to have a vehicle. They seriously frowned upon using a mechanic not on the compound. More isolation.

Boys sports that was limited to those staff kids and only those willing
To prove worthy by totally submitting and accepting their twisted ideologies.

When someone screams at you from a pulpit weekly, telling you unless you believe how they do, your doomed to hell as a worthless piece of garbage, you eventually begin to think you are.

We lived in the crap trailers past the air strip. Mind you Roloff lived in a plush house while his workers lived in crap.

One of the celebrations when they used Separation of Church and state as a reason to not answer to the state for all the abuse and sexual assaults done by staff. It was practicing their version of their religion.

ABOUT THE AUTHOR

An Author, Journalist, Commentator, and Activist with a voice to speak out against abuse, I felt compelled to help share other's stories of survival. I too am a survivor. I grew up in a strict Fundamentalist home. I began to rebel. This left me on a plane en-route to what would be the first of many religion based reform homes that would change my life forever.

A total of several years in and out of Fundamentalist reform homes, I discovered what it was like to lose my identity and always feel that death would be my only salvation. I learned the ultimate submission of will, all in the name of self-sacrifice to their cause. Raped and abused and without a sense of ability to function as an adult mentally, I finally did escape an immature adult into a world I was not prepared for.

A few decades have passed, and although it has been a long road of growing up, learning from my mistakes, I have discovered my past experiences have made me who I am today, an activist with a voice. I Share my voice, the voices of others and this book to enlighten and educate people of what can happen behind the sacred walls of some of the facilities still open all over the United States.